First published in 2007 by Cherrytree Books,
a division of the Evans Publishing Group
2A Portman Mansions
Chiltern St
London W1U 6NR

Design. D.R.ink

British Library Cataloguing in Publication Data
Amos, Janine
      Liar – (Good & Bad Series)
      I. Title II. Green, Gwen III. Series
      177.3

ISBN 1 84234 395 5
13 –digit ISBN (from 1 Jan 2007) 978 1 84234 395 1

Liar

By Janine Amos

Illustrated by Gwen Green

CHERRYTREE BOOKS

Kerry's story

It was the last day of term. Everyone was talking about the summer holidays.

"We're going camping in France," said Louise.

"I'm going to stay with my granddad," said Peter. "He lives on a farm."

"My granddad lives in a castle," said Kerry, pushing her way into the group. "We stay there every summer. It's got huge towers, and my bedroom's right at the top."

Everyone was listening, so Kerry went on. "Then we'll go on another holiday. We'll probably go to Disneyland. I'll sleep in a big hotel – and eat popcorn – and stay there for ages." Kerry stopped to take a breath.

"I've got a new bikini to wear on holiday," said Louise.

"I've got a new sweatshirt," said Kim.

"I've got loads of new clothes," said Kerry.

"I bet you haven't got trainers like these," said Daniel, waggling his foot.

"I've got two pairs," said Kerry quickly, "but I'm not allowed to wear them until the holidays. And I've got a ball gown to wear at the castle."

Kerry wasn't quite sure what a ball gown was – but it sounded just right.

Do you think Kerry is telling the truth?

Soon it was home time.

"Have a good summer, everyone!" called Kerry's teacher.

Kerry's head was full of castles and Disneyland. She was almost at the school gate – then she remembered her bag.

"I'll have to go back for it," thought Kerry.

Kerry pushed open the classroom door. Then she heard voices – and she heard her own name.

"I don't believe Kerry's going to Disneyland," Daniel was saying.

"She's always making things up," said Louise.

"Her granddad doesn't live in a castle," said Kim. "He lives in a bungalow near us!"

Everyone laughed. Kerry went red. She was glad that they couldn't see her.

"That Kerry's a liar!" said Peter.

How do you think Kerry feels

Kerry didn't stop for her bag. She ran all the way home. Her feet hit the pavement hard. "Liar! Liar!" they seemed to say, over and over again.

When Kerry got home she was crying.

"Calm down, Kerry," said her dad. "Tell me what's wrong."

"I haven't got any friends," sobbed Kerry. "They're all talking about me. They said I'm a liar."

Kerry told her dad what had happened. He listened carefully.

"Why do you make up these stories?" he asked.

Kerry didn't answer.

"Is it to make people listen?" said her dad. "Is it to make you the centre of attention?"

Kerry nodded. "I suppose so," she said slowly. "I think of something interesting to say. Then the idea grows and grows."

"And you get carried away," smiled her dad.

Kerry's dad put his arm round her.

"Life's not a competition," he said. "You don't have to pretend to do amazing things. People will like you for yourself."

Kerry looked up at him. "But what will I tell everyone after the holidays?" she asked.

"They'll forget all about it over the summer," said her dad.

"You can go back to school and talk about what you really did."

Is Kerry's dad right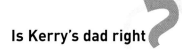

Feeling like Kerry

Have you ever felt like Kerry? Have you ever made things up to get attention? Making things up can become a habit. You might find you do it more and more. You might find that others stop believing you.

Changing the truth

We all change the truth a bit sometimes. We might build up a true story to make it funnier. It makes life more exciting. Lies like this don't hurt anyone. But it's important not to overdo it. You could end up hurting yourself, like Kerry.

No one likes a liar

Has anyone ever lied to you? It doesn't feel good, does it? It makes you feel silly – or cross – or unsure. No one likes a liar. And, as Kerry found, no one likes someone who pretends to be better than everyone else.

Think about it

Read the stories in this book. Think about the people in the stories. You might feel like them sometimes. If you feel like telling a lie try thinking about it first. And try telling the truth instead.

Ben's story

It was break time. Everyone was meant to be in the playground. But Ben was playing in the classroom with some other boys.

"Shh, Ben!" called Joseph. "Mr Blake will hear us. He'll make us go outside."

Ben wasn't listening. "Look at me! I'm a pirate!" he shouted, waving a ruler.

Just then there was a crash. Ben had knocked over the water jug on Mr Blake's desk. Water spilled everywhere.

Joseph and the others ran off. Ben looked at the mess. There was a big puddle on the pile of exercise books. He tried to mop it up with his sleeve.

"Mr Blake will go mad," thought Ben.

Suddenly the classroom door opened. It was Mr Blake! He saw the mess straightaway.

"Just look at my desk!" shouted the teacher. "What happened?"

Ben didn't know what to say. Then he had an idea.

"It was Joseph and Billy," said Ben. "They were fighting. They knocked over your jug."

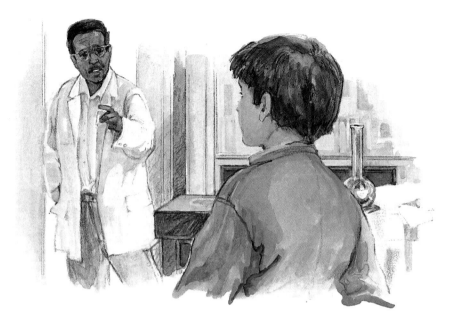

Mr Blake gave Ben a long look.

"What are you doing inside, anyway?" he asked. "You're meant to be in the playground at break."

Ben turned away. He was thinking fast.

"It's my leg. I hurt it playing football. I came in to sit down," he lied. "That's when I saw Joseph and Billy fighting."

"Wait until I find those boys!" said Mr Blake, dashing off.

How many lies has Ben told
Why didn't he tell the truth

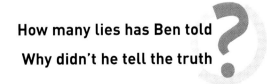

Ben waited in the empty classroom. He could hear the drip, drip of the water running onto the floor. Ben thought about Joseph and Billy. He wondered what would happen. Ben started to get worried.

What do you think will happen?

At last break was over. The whole of Ben's class came running back. Joseph and Billy came in behind the others, with Mr Blake. Billy looked upset. Joseph looked cross. They both stared at Ben.

"Ben's a liar!" shouted Joseph. "He knocked over the water – not us!"

Ben went bright red.

"Is this true, Ben?" asked Mr Blake.

Ben nodded.

"And did you lie about hurting your leg, too?" asked the teacher.

"Yes," whispered Ben.

How does Ben feel now

And how do you think Joseph and Billy feel

All afternoon Ben worked on his own. He knew the others were talking about him. He heard them whisper, "Liar!" as he walked past.

Ben couldn't do his sums. He couldn't think properly. Ben wanted the lesson to hurry up and finish. He wanted to go home.

At last school was over for the day. Ben walked up to Mr Blake's desk.

"I'm sorry," said Ben quietly. "I'm sorry I spilt the water. And I'm sorry I told lies."

"Accidents happen," said his teacher. "But there's no excuse for lying."

Mr Blake looked at Ben, and Ben looked down at his feet.

"I don't like being lied to, Ben," said Mr Blake. "Can I trust you in future?"

"Yes," nodded Ben. "Being a liar feels terrible," he said.

Feeling like Ben

Ben told lies because he was scared of being told off. But, as Mr Blake said, people will forgive an accident. It's harder to forgive a lie – because it's done on purpose.

Lies spread

Ben started by telling one lie. Soon he'd told another. Once you've told one lie, you may think you need to tell more. You may need to cover up your first lie. And it gets harder to tell the truth.

Ruth's story

Ruth was sitting in the kitchen. Outside the sky was grey. It had been raining all morning. Ruth could smell lunch cooking. But she wasn't very hungry. She started to kick her feet against the table. Ruth knew that it annoyed her mum.

"Stop that, please, Ruth," said Ruth's mum.

"It's my birthday next week," said Ruth.

"I know," said her mum.

"Will Dad come home for my party?" asked Ruth.

Ruth's mum carried on with the washing up. "You know he won't, Ruthie," she said. "He'll send you a present and a card."

Ruth didn't want a present and a card – she wanted her dad.

But he didn't live there any more.

The next day, Ruth was at the pool with her friends.

"It's your party on Saturday," said Joy.

"Last year you had a great party," said Jess. "Your dad did all those magic tricks."

Ruth remembered last year's party. Her dad had put on a funny hat. He'd made everyone laugh. Ruth wriggled her toes in the water.

"Will he do some magic this year?" asked Jess.

Ruth thought about her dad, miles away in his new flat.

"Yes," she said slowly. "He's learnt lots of new tricks – just for my birthday. He's been practising for weeks."

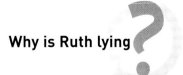

Why is Ruth lying

"He's got loads of new jokes to tell, too," Ruth went on.

"Tell us one now. Go on, Ruth," said Joy.

"You'll have to wait until Saturday," said Ruth.

Ruth wanted to cry. She ducked under the water and splashed about. She didn't want the others to see her face.

How do you think Ruth feels?

All week, Ruth tried not to think about her party. But people kept asking her questions.

"Who's coming?" Jess wanted to know.

"What are you going to wear?" asked Joy.

"Would you like takeaway pizza on Saturday?" asked Ruth's mum.

"I don't care," snapped Ruth.

Ruth didn't want Saturday to come. She was scared.

Why is Ruth scared?

What do you think she will do?

On Saturday, Ruth was late getting up.

"Come on, Birthday Girl!" said her mum.

"I don't feel well," said Ruth. "I can't have a party. Will you telephone everyone?"

Ruth's mum sat down next to her on the bed.

"Is it because Dad won't be here?" asked Ruth's mum quietly.

"Sort of," nodded Ruth. She told her mum everything she'd said to Jess and Joy. "And when they get here, they'll know I'm a liar," finished Ruth sadly.

"You haven't been very bad, Ruth," said her mum. "You just talked about the things you wished would happen."

Ruth's mum gave her a big hug.

"You're still getting used to Dad living somewhere else," she said. "So am I. It means our lives will change."

"But I don't want things to change," said Ruth.

"It's hard, I know," her mum said. "But we have to face up to the truth. Lying doesn't help."

"It just gets things muddled," agreed Ruth.

Slowly, Ruth got out of bed.

"What shall I tell everyone?" she asked.

"Tell them the truth. Tell them that your dad's not here – that you wished he would come, but he isn't going to," said her mum.

Ruth started to get dressed. "This year's party will be different," she said.

"But it will still be good," smiled her mum.

"Is there takeaway pizza?" asked Ruth, looking up.

"You bet!" said Ruth's mum, laughing.

How does Ruth feel now

How did Ruth's mum help

Feeling like Ruth?

Ruth told lies because she didn't like the truth. She told her friends things she wished were true instead. But that didn't help. It only made her scared.

When truth hurts

Have you ever told lies, like Ruth? Have you ever made up stories because the truth hurts? It may feel easier to pretend that things are all right when they're not. It may feel easier to keep bad things secret. But lies and secrets don't help. The truth won't go away.

Talking helps

Facing up to the truth can be painful. You may need help. Talk to an adult you trust. Talking about things helped Ruth. It can help you, too.

Thinking about lying

Kerry, Ben and Ruth each told lies. And they each learnt something about lying. Think about the stories in this book. What have you learnt about lying – and about telling the truth?

If you are feeling frightened or unhappy, don't keep it to yourself. Talk to an adult you can trust, like a parent or a teacher. If you feel really alone, you could telephone or write to one of these offices. Remember, there is always someone who can help.

Childline
Freephone 0800 1111
Address: Freepost 1111, London N1 0BR
www.childline.org.uk

Childline for children in care
Freephone 0800 884444 (6 - 10pm)

NSPCC Child Protection Line
Freephone 0808 8005000
www.nspcc.org.uk

The Samaritans
08457 909090
www.samaritans.org.uk